Paper Quilling Book for Beginners

A Guide to Craft 20 Stylish Paper Quilling Patterns, Designs and Quilling Projects with Step by Step Instructions, Plus Tools and Techniques Included

By

Angelica Lipsey

Copyright © 2021 – Angelica Lipsey

All rights reserved

No part of this publication may be reproduced, distributed, or transmitted in any form or by any means, including photocopying, recording, or other electronic or mechanical methods, without the prior written permission of the publisher, except in the case of brief quotations embodied in reviews and certain other non-commercial uses permitted by copyright law.

Disclaimer

This publication is designed to provide competent and reliable information regarding the subject matter covered. However, the views expressed in this publication are those of the author alone, and should not be taken as expert instruction or professional advice. The reader is responsible for his or her own actions.

The author hereby disclaims any responsibility or liability whatsoever that is incurred from the use or application of the contents of this publication by the purchaser or reader. The purchaser or reader is hereby responsible for his or her own actions.

Table of Contents

Introduction 7

Chapter 1 8

The Basics of Paper Quilling 8

    What is Paper Quilling? 8

    History of Paper Quilling 9

    Benefits of Paper Quilling 10

    Application Areas of Paper Quilling 15

Chapter 2 19

Common Terms Used in Paper Quilling 19

Chapter 3 27

Tips and Techniques in Paper Quilling 27

Chapter 4 40

Getting Started with Paper Quilling 40

    Tools and Materials Needed 40

        Paper Quilling Strips 40
        Quilling Needle 43

    Craft Knife 44
    Craft Glue 45
    Cutting Mat 46
    Scissors 48
    Tweezers 48
    Ruler 49
    Circular Ruler 50
    Sealers 51
Cutting Paper Quilling Strips 52

Basic Paper Quilling Shapes 56

Chapter 5 69

Paper Quilling Project Ideas 69

  Photo Frame 69

  Easy Fashionable Quilled Angel 73

  Teardrop Vase 76

  Quilled Easter Egg Design 80

  Fall Tree 83

  Hedgehog 87

  Bats 91

  Wreath Ornament 95

Flower Garden 97

Watermelon Jewelry 101

Flower Cake 103

Snowflakes 106

Flower Basket 109

Paper Quilled Tops 113

Monogram 115

Reindeer 119

Candy Cane 121

3D Corrugated Flowers 122

Turkey Design 125

Shamrock Card 128

3D Snowman Design 131

New Year Quilling Greeting Card 133

Chapter 6 137

Resolving Paper Quilling Common Mistakes 137

Chapter 7 144

Paper Quilling Frequently Asked Questions 144

Conclusion 150

Introduction

In recent times, paper quilling is beginning to dominate the art world globally. The process of quilling is also referred to as paper filigree. It is the making use of shaped paper strips to create beautiful paper quilling designs.

The paper used for these designs is curled, looped, rolled, and twisted to create shapes, giving way for attractive designs. Paper Quilling didn't start today as it was in existence since the 15th century.

The shaped design made from paper quilling is used to decorate boxes, design picture frames, make 3D stand-alone art pieces and boxes. Also, intending and current paper quillers should be aware that paper quilling projects can either appear simple or complex.

However, it would help if you didn't get scared because the art of paper quilling can be learned and practiced in less than 3 hours. Paper quilling is the best art project for beginners and professionals because it doesn't involve too many materials and thinking.

Get into the art of designing paper quilling projects with this guide, and you'll be glad you did so.

Chapter 1

The Basics of Paper Quilling

What is Paper Quilling?

Paper quilling involves the process of cutting paper into long thin shreds, rolling and making the paper parts into diverse shapes, and joining the shapes to create beautiful art. The result from paper quilling is mostly used to beautify gifts, cards, picture frames, 3D artworks, and boxes.

In paper quilling, your negative thoughts are the only thing that reduces the possibility of decorating beautiful arts. You can choose to create the paper quilling art, simple or complex. As a beginner, one or two hours is the least time for you to learn and prepare a wonderful and attractive paper quilling design.

The quilled strips in paper quilling can be joined onto a thick piece of canvas or cardstock. Additionally, you can also glue the quilled strips onto objects like boxes to create jewelry.

History of Paper Quilling

The beginning of paper quilling can be traced to as far back as the 15th century. At that time, paper quilling was used by the French and Italian nuns to beautify religious objects like crosses and books.

The Italians and French would usually use paper strips taken from the edges of covered books to form an excellent quilled artwork.

In the 18th century, paper quilling began to make waves, and it was seen in other parts of Europe. In fact, it became increasingly popular with women referred to as "ladies of leisure." This term was used to mean women who are not under the bondage of work and women who are not forced to carry out specific responsibilities.

As time went on, Paper quilling extended to the United States when the North American country was colonized. However, quilling began losing its value worldwide when other arts like drawing, manufacturing jewelry, and sewing began to emerge.

In modern times, paper quilling is gradually making a massive comeback. This is primarily due to widespread social media and the chance for the world to share and find new decorative arts.

Benefits of Paper Quilling

Paper quilling can be a stress-free and straightforward hobby, and it serves its benefits to humans. For some individuals, they have dedicated one room to store and make more beautiful papercrafts.

But what makes paper quilling an exciting hobby? The hobby is an easy one, and you don't have to spend too much money to decorate a papercraft. You only need to lay your hands on the required materials, and within a few hours, you would be done with a particular papercraft.

Anything you can form or make using paper can be termed paper quilling, and you stand a lot to gain from making the craft. Paper quilling allows us to take our minds away from the harsh condition of the world we live in.

Also, it shows us that we can be happy designing papercrafts. We have compiled the several benefits of paper quilling in the list below:

1. It boosts our creativity level

Paper quilling is a perfect way of increasing and boosting our creativity level. It is also a great way to show others how creative we can be with paper. With paper quilling, you have tons of choices from textures, shapes, and colors.

Once we can be exceptional in creating beautiful paper quilling designs, our creativity level will increase and blend into our everyday life. If our creativity level is high, we will not find it challenging to solve issues that emanate from life itself.

Creativity is a skill on its own, and it is a talent that can only be built and maintained with hobbies such as designing papercrafts.

2. It allows us to express ourselves

Are you feeling tensed or worried? Paper quilling allows you to express your emotions without feeling down. Once you complete a paper quilling project, you will feel happy because you can finish a task.

Also, you can express anything you are feeling on your paper quilling project. For example, if you are happy, the result of your excitement will show in the papercraft you are designing. The same thing applies to when you are sad or when you are feeling in-between happy and dejected.

3. Meditate and Relax

With paper quilling as an option, you can easily take some time off from work or operating your technological devices. In fact, paper quilling also allows you to take a break, breathe, and enjoy others' art of designing something.

Paper quilling is proven to assist people with their state of mind. Take origami craft, for example; once you understand the process of folding by heart, the origami craft can make you focus all your attention on it, thereby making you meditate and relax.

The ability to focus on something is a great way to focus and relax from other pressing things. Paper craft's kind of meditation has proven to soothe and steady the mind and promote serenity.

4. Boost your self-esteem

There are several responsibilities and jobs we are meant to complete regularly, but only a few of these jobs result in things we can see. The opportunity we have to see and know the task we are doing helps our disturbed minds to look at the things we had done, especially when we started it ourselves.

Upon completing a particular papercraft, we feel fulfilled and pleased, thereby boosting our self-esteem. Being able to be confident about completing a task is enough reason to have high self-esteem.

5. It enhances our mental and motor skills

Research has shown that involving in paper quilling and other hand tasks improve several parts of the brain and help us handle things easily.

Virtually every paper quilling task or hands-on tasks involves mental work such as deciding where to place a gum or putting the different materials. Following the movements of accurate directions while engaging in a hobby like paper quilling helps improve our mental skills.

In addition, paper quilling also helps us develop hand-eye organization skills that won't negatively affect our physical health. As a result, this benefit makes paper quilling helpful for the old regarding body and mind.

A study found in the Journal of Neuropsychiatry revealed that reading books, engaging in paper quilling, and playing games could reduce our likelihood of developing minor rational deficiencies by 30% to 50%.

6. Create and fortify bonds

Paper quilling is a great task which allows you to involve your entire family members, from the young ones to the old ones. Paper crafts are also a great activity you can use to strengthen the bonds of friends who are far apart from each other.

Asides from friends and family members, paper crafts also help us find and know more of your community members. If you want to make new friends, you can enroll in any paper quilling class or group online or in any craft store around.

One exciting thing about paper quilling and bonding with friends and family members is that they all share the same thoughts of decorating unique and beautiful paper designs. No one will be left out from the idea of coming together to make well-crafted designs.

Since everyone shares the same idea as you, it would be very difficult for the bond to break, especially if you would regularly decorate papers with them.

7. Reuse and recycle

There is more than enough happiness to derive from reusing something over again. In fact, you will also derive satisfaction from knowing that you can reuse something that will come out very beautiful.

Used papers are still beneficial, and they can be used to make attractive paper designs. In our world today, we are always searching for methods to increase the worth of things we do not need.

As an art or crafty individual, you may have stored lots of old art projects because of their beautiful state and because you feel they might be useful at a later time. Recycling is a hobby that makes paper crafts so loved and used by several people worldwide.

Application Areas of Paper Quilling

Paper quilling serves different purposes to individuals and groups in the craft world. It can be applied to virtually everything you can imagine. Paper quilling designs are mostly found during the festive period and another jubilating/exciting period like Easter.

Check below to see the various uses of paper quilling:

1. **It can be used to decorate cards**

Perhaps your loved one or someone close to you has his or her birthday in a couple of days. You can easily spend two or three hours of your time decorating near-perfect and beautiful paper quilled cards.

There are tons of paper quilled cards you can design with written letters that will wow the birthday celebrant. Paper quill cards are designed for birthday celebrants and people who need to be sent a loving message through a card.

2. It can be used to decorate picture frames

If you have done a picture frame before and want to beautify it more, you may want to consider using a paper quilling frame design.

Designing a paper quilling frame is a simple process, and with the steps at your disposal, you can easily create a paper quilling frame. The designed picture frame can even be presented as a gift to someone or kept in your home for beauty purposes.

3. It can be used to decorate boxes

Want to give someone a big or small box for a special occasion? You can use an attractive paper quilling design on the box and present it to that special person of yours.

Beautifully designed boxes offer a sense of love and affection between you and the other person.

4. It can be used to design earrings

Nothing can be more fulfilling than making your personal earrings, right? You may want to add to your earring's beauty by designing a special paper quilled earring as a lady. These designed earrings can be worn on your ear and taken to special occasions like birthdays, weddings, and parties.

Most people may be unable to distinguish between a proper earring and a quilled paper earring.

5. It can be used to decorate your home

Without attaching the paper quilling design to anything else, you can easily design a beautiful paper quilling project and hang it on your wall to serve its different purposes.

For example, during the Christmas season, you can design a paper quilling Christmas project and hang it on your door or close to your Christmas tree. People passing by or entering your home will see that you celebrate the Christmas season in grand style.

6. It can be made as a 3D stand-alone art piece

3D stand-alone art pieces are designs made in the form of someone else. For example, during the USA's Christmas season, you may choose to design a 3D stand-alone snowman and place the designed piece at the front of your door.

The designed paper quilled snowman will send numerous messages to passersby and those who will join you in celebrating the season. 3D stand-alone art pieces can come in different forms. You can design or draw someone using a paper quill and present it to the person anytime you want.

Chapter 2

Common Terms Used in Paper Quilling

Are you a paper quilling beginner? Do you want to enter into the excitement of designing different projects? Why not start with understanding the various terms used in paper quilling?

The various terms used in paper quilling will broaden your paper quilling understanding and help you gain knowledge of everything that concerns paper quilling.

Here are some of the common terms used in paper quilling:

1. **Border Buddy:** You should make paper rings of various sizes for a quilling plan and afterward fill it later. A border body encourages you to make the base ring shape. Dowel Forms and Stacked Quilling Forms are other options to consider asides from Border Buddy.

2. **Needle Tool:** The needle tool is comfortable when you need to make more little coils and centers. You need to curl the paper around the needle and begin rolling it to create a coil. Once you understand how to do this very well, you can create additional small coils.

3. **Paper Crimper:** Paper crimper is also referred to as quilling winder. It is used to design a paper strip with a zig-zag shape. The free coiled paper crimper is then used to make long strip shapes.

4. **Quilling Coach:** A quilling coach is typically used alongside the slotted tool. It aids you in holding the paper strip and effectively wind it into an enormous coil. Its level surface keeps the loop complete and keeps it from loosening up out of the blue. A quilling coach is particularly helpful for youthful quillers, as their little hands regularly need some additional help.

5. **Quilling Comb:** Quilled floral crafts frequently expect you to make sophisticated laced loops (otherwise called husking). These are produced by using a quilling comb. The quilling comb is small and spaced, and it contains fine metal poles to assist you with making unending patterns with at least one paper strip.

6. **Quilling Guides:** A quilling guide has frameworks with concentric circles stamped on its surface. It helps you make a quilled object with an even plan, such as a 6-pointed flower or an 8-pointed snowflake. The grid guide likewise proves to be useful for husking and adjusting your paper strips while interlacing or knitting them to form one.

7. **Quilling Molds:** Most Quillers use molds for making 3D quilled designs and quilled jewelry. When you make a tight loop with an ordinary quilling tool, just place it on the ideal form size and position the paper below to apply the shape.

8. **Quilling Paper Strips:** Quilling paper is majorly available to utilize portions of various colors and widths. Most used paper strips sizes are 3mm and 5mm; nonetheless, more extensive sizes of 7mm and 10mm are likewise accessible. It is anything but difficult to use strips of these sizes using a slotted tool. Narrow strips are made for better quilling designs and more extensive strips for 3D quilling craft and bordered flowers.

9. **Sizing Boards:** A measuring/sizing board or work board causes you to make entirely round coils of wanted sizes and even coils with uneven circles. Simply roll the paper strip and position it in the open space of the ideal size and shape. Its lower side is usually produced from cork, so they are likely to hold leveled pins used to cover the quilled shapes. You can purchase sizing boards in different sizes and shapes.

10. **Slotted Tool:** A slotted tool lets you position the paper strip's edge inside the space and fold it easily. The slotted tool is best used for learners and experts

11. **Straight Pins:** Most quillers use straight pins on worksheets to close or cover the coils. Straight pins are essential to your quilling project as you can change the quilled shape before using glue, and the exterior quilled shape will remain as it is.

12. **Tweezers:** This is one of many essential tools that should be in your quilling pack. A pair of tweezers can assist you in positioning the paper, holding the coil, and gluing it. Tweezers may come in curved or straight formats. The Straight Tweezer has a long and even point tip, though the curved tweezers feature a titled one. Tweezers are also very helpful to most crafters for dealing with different undertakings.

13. **Shiner/Top Coat:** A Top Coat/Shiner goes about as a defensive layer on your quilled design and helps fend off dirt and moisture. Depending on the method you seek to achieve, different coats might be used.

14. **Paper Bead Tool:** The paper bead tool is like the slotted tool and allows you to make different shapes. Obviously, the likelihood of the shape size relies on the paper cut. Notwithstanding, this tool can hold a few pieces of paper and even paper with more extensive cuts.

15. **Needle Forms:** Needle forms allow you to make little paper rings of different sizes. These structures are profoundly helpful if you want to create a piece of quilled jewelry.

16. **Cookie Cutters:** This tool has several shapes and permits you to offer part of your paper strip by

directing it around the cutter. The cookie-cutter additionally keeps the strip in an assigned space.

17. **Quillography or On-edge Quilling:** Quillography quilling is similar to 3D typography. Craft designers will have to use card stock and afterward create the layout of the letterforms. You can additionally change its shape according to your creative senses.

18. **Quilled Mosaics:** Quilled mosaics are wonderful art designs produced with the use of extensive paper strips. Quillers make basic shapes with a layout of a similar color and merge them to frame a mosaic.

19. **3-D Quilling:** When a quilled design project isn't stuck to the page and is preferably positioned, it seems to stand upward in a three-dimensional way. 3D quilling is done with more extensive and thicker paper strips. Some examples of quilled items include boxes, animals, and wedding cake toppers.

20. **Husking:** Husking is a strategy of quilling paper strips into circles for creating petals. This sort of quilling needs you to use a grid guide and straight pins.

21. **Bordering Scissors:** These particularly designed scissors feature five sharp edges, allowing you to make bordered flowers.

Chapter 3

Tips and Techniques in Paper Quilling

Paper Quilling Tips

Paper quilling is the art of rolling paper into twists or folding papers into curls and organizing them to make multidimensional layers.

In the past, quilling used to be extraordinarily popular in the 1970s and '80s, and little by little, it made a breathtaking bounce back in the later time. Paper quilling is unquestionably not a demanding hobby or career to explore- you can finish a project in some minutes.

Here we've assembled several tips quilling beginners will value:

1. Quilling Paper

Quilling paper is, without a doubt, the key material for a quilling project. Even though you can purchase strips of pre-cut, colorful quilling paper from craft and art stores, you could likewise use PC paper and pieces any paper to start, which includes superbly colored junk mail. The two efficient tips to kick you off are:

- Begin by selecting a paper-quilling guide to fully understand and know the size and length of the paper you need.

- Let us assume you do not have colored paper; you can color the coils equally once you conclude the arrangements.

2. The Quilling Tools

On the part of the tool you will need for quilling, a slotted tool is ideal for starters due to its simplicity. However, if you want to prevent the tool's crease on your completed paper strips, select the needle tool.

Other supplies for paper quilling you need to include are as follows:

- Glue

- A work-board

- A couple of tweezers to select and move around the quilled pieces

- Circle layout for measuring the loops

3. Start with basic shapes

The basic shapes are the most important, so you need to start with them. One significant example of a basic shape is the rolled round paper twist. To make different shapes such as the paisley, tear, slug, marquis, or tulip, ensure you develop this basic shape. Until you acquire the quilled shape you want, continue to pound, crush, and modify the weight.

Here are a couple of helpful tips for making the fundamental or basic rolled paper coil:

- Place a tiny paper strip into the opening of your tool, and afterward, use your thumb and forefinger on one or the other side of the paper strip. Then while you change the position, simply use a strain to hold it.

- Take the paper off the tool when you get to the end of your paper strip. Ensure you don't wind it too firmly because you may discover it somewhat interesting to take it off the tool.

- Let us assume you intend to make a free coil shape; allowing the paper coil to extend before eliminating it from the tool is the best option. However, if you need a closer twist, do not allow it to grow before taking it off.

4. Go past the shapes

Whenever you have made the intriguing shapes, feel free to mess with them. You have the option of;

- Using them to adorn a welcome card
- Making hand-made and appealing jewelry
- Creating or designing a framed craftsmanship
- Creating three-dimensional miniatures and figures

One of the simplest quilling projects that can be of assistance to you is making a flower. These methods listed below should be followed properly:

- To create the center of the flower, simply cut two thin strips of colored quilling paper. Cut an extensive strip, double the more slender strips' width, especially for the flower petals.

- Use a quilling needle or toothpick to make a firm roll of the more slender strip. The end part of the strip should be glued.

- In another thin strip, simply add glue before moving it around the initial roll. To make a firmly rolled center for the flower, simply glue the end of the strip.

- Proceed to create cuts up and down the more extensive strip, mostly down its breadth. Include glues to one finish of the strip and roll it around the firmly rolled flower.

- Glue the finish of the strip that appears wide. When the glue is dried, use your thumb and fingers to fold the petals on the outer part.

5. Join it with other art

To make fascinating pieces of a gift, simply use your quilt shapes and other works of art, especially those on paper. You can utilize your quilled shapes to:

- Paint and decorate walls

- Decorate paper holders

- Hand-made jewelry boxes

6. Utilize the accessible assets

Many book shops have available paper quilling guides and instructions. Beginners of all ages can begin with books composed for kids that have fantastic guidelines. Also, kid's paper quilling books are simple and straightforward to read.

You can also get to read exciting paper quilling books on the internet through blogs and websites.

7. Not a viable alternative for training

Indeed, practice is the catchphrase. Similar to other art, paper quilling needs a lot of training to learn the skill. So, assuming you need to quill like the masters, you need to practice as regularly as you are reasonably expected to. Attempt more intricate shapes and creative patterns if you want to master the quilling craft.

NOTE: If you have kids at home, quilling is an excellent method and exciting way to keep the little ones locked in.

Paper Quilling Techniques

While quilling is rapidly becoming popular, it's still elusive to other people who practice the art. Artists consistently depend on the insight of more educated crafters to show us the little techniques they know. If there are not too many quillers worldwide, how then do you expect to master the art of paper quilling?

It is often difficult for new quillers to enter the art stage and stake a claim to the globe. However, there shouldn't be a cause for alarm because we have compiled several techniques that will help most beginner paper quillers transition to being professional quillers.

1. Colors portray your quilling

Applying glue to colorful coils to a white background can be stunning when designing a typography plan.

However, in a mosaic, a white background is an interruption.

There are many things to notice in art designed quilled shapes, and the eye will generally be attracted to the difference that background makes. Use a colored background to assist viewers in seeing the things you want to focus on.

2. Use thread snippers, not scissors

Large scissors can discomfort you when designing a paper quill (both in a real sense and metaphorically). Most tasks require a great deal of cutting, and the heaviness of scissors can cause torment in your wrist.

Select a lightweight pair of string snippers from the sewing parts of your neighborhood craft store instead. They are ideal for clipping off the glue-bound closures of quilling paper, and they can easily enter a quilling toolbox.

3. Get an ideal center in all coils

Everybody needs perfect coils; however, quilling with a needle tool is increasingly slow than with a slotted tool. Fortunately, there are a few different ways to accomplish an entirely round center, sans crimping, using a slotted tool.

The best strategy is to continue turning your quilling tool after you have arrived at the end of your strip until you believe the tool allows you. Tool tears the little bit of paper that would have been the crimp, and you will have a perfect coil. Supposing your quilling tool can't bear to turn as it should, nonetheless, a piercing tool or pin can smoothen the crimp.

4. Tear rather than cut

Most people prefer clean lines and concealing all seams when they can. However, some of the time, there's no place to cover up. If you don't care for the appearance of paper seams, you can tear the end of your quilling strip instead of cutting it with scissors to reduce the likely effect.

5. Roll with and not against the quilling strip's edge

Whenever you cut a quilling paper, the blade edge cuts from the top and in descending order. This makes both of the long edges somewhat rolled downwards. It's so minor, truth be told, that's difficult to see without the help of a recommended glass, yet you can feel it when the strip is run between your fingers.

It would be best to roll with the curve for a more amazing coil: the descending curve should look down. It's somewhat precarious to catch when you first attempt (and it isn't fundamental to attractive quilling); however, if you focus well, it will turn out to be nearly instinctual.

6. Use a needle structure before a quilling comb

Most craft quillers believe quilling comb wastes their time, and it is not straightforward. One basic technique to keep you going is to use a needle form before deciding to use a quilling comb.

Here's what you should do: Roll a small bit coil with a quilling needle form and send it to your quilling comb and design your preferred shape. Once this can be done, the center of your coil will be perfect.

7. Double up your strips for a grippy roll

In some instances, you may be needed to roll a massive coil, and most times, the middle will be loose from the quilling tool. The sole option you can take is to roll the rest of it using your hand.

However, you can prevent this from occurring by doubling up the strip to begin your coil. The process of doubling up your strips will keep everything as it should. The alternative is to use two stops over each other or fold your first strip on the other's top.

8. Use nippers to fix your slip-ups

On the whole, most craft quillers make an honest effort to make each coil great. They cautiously watch their glue and match up the seams as well as they can. However, they can't all be great. This is where this tip of using nipper to fix your slip-ups comes into play.

You are expected to use cuticle nippers to cut off a crooked edge. It can even be used to remove undesirable glue that has dried. The cuticle nippers can be purchased at any drug store.

9. Sponges are a quillers closest companion

This innovative arrangement is excellent, and it works twofold. You can use a container to hold the tip of your needle glue bottle on the other side to guarantee that it's all set whenever you have a reason to use it again.

If you soaked the sponge before usage, it would keep your glue from drying and obstructing the tip.

Furthermore, you can use the sponge's surface to remove any glue that sticks to your fingers.

To design yours, simply tear out a sponge and place it in a little dish.

10. An eye pin gets the job done without failing

This technique is ideal for people who left their cap off, and their used needle tip is blocked. The mistake is not a grievous one because you can always correct it. An eye pin is an ideal answer for removing the tip so you can return to designing your paper quilling project.

It has a blunt edge that makes it secure than using a sewing pin. Simply try not to leave it in the tip for quite a while because the pin is likely to rust and stain your glue.

These listed ten paper quilling techniques will help you in your journey to becoming a quilling professional.

A Short message from the Author:

Hey, I hope you are enjoying the book? I would love to hear your thoughts!

Many readers do not know how hard reviews are to come by and how much they help an author.

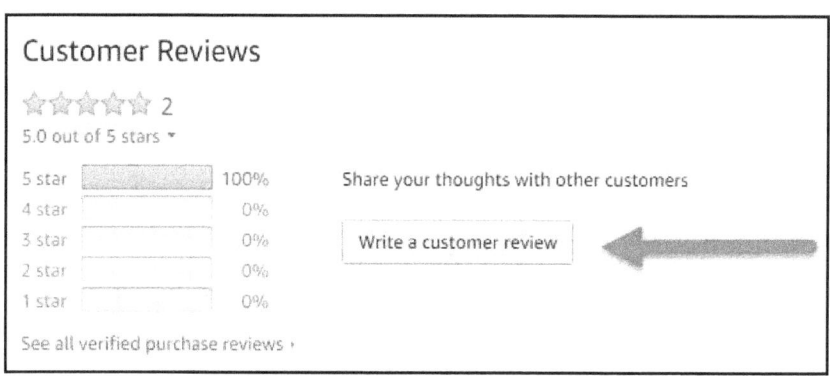

I would be incredibly grateful if you could take just 60 seconds to write a short review on Amazon, even if it is a few sentences!

>> Click here to leave a quick review

Thanks for the time taken to share your thoughts!

Chapter 4

Getting Started with Paper Quilling

Tools and Materials Needed

Paper Quilling Strips

Paper is fundamental in quilling, and a paper quilling project cannot be done without paper strips. You can either purchase pre-cut paper strips or physically cut the pieces yourself. There are advantages and disadvantages to the two sorts of paper strips with pre-cut paper saving time and energy yet being more expensive than DIY paper strips.

Pre-Cut Paper Strips for Quilling

You can purchase quilled paper in pre-cut strips saving you time and energy from measuring and cutting papers. Quilling kits for beginners typically incorporate pre-cut strips. Most people prefer to use pre-cut paper strips for their actual quilling. Also, pre-cut paper strips are sold in craft stores.

With pre-cut paper, you'll have the option to ensure that your strips will be the right paper type and weight with smooth and equal edges. Although there is no assurance your pre-cut paper will have the correct size, but it is something you can try out. Pre-sliced paper likewise is also acid-free, guaranteeing that the strips won't stain over long periods. Strips are typically accessible in widths of 1/16 – 1 inch, so if you want a size outside that range, you may need to fall back on cutting your strips.

DIY Paper Strips for Quilling

You will save money and time if you cut paper strips yourself. The interesting thing here is that you can use extra paper from other artworks to cut your paper strips.

You will likewise have the opportunity to use paper that differs in gradient, patterns, or texture. Usually, the pre-cut paper will be accessible in lovely standard intense colors. Beginners should begin with pre-cut paper strips so that they can enjoy the craft.

The Most Effective Method to Make Your Paper Strips

There are two distinct approaches to make your paper strips: mechanical or manual. The mechanical technique needs a shredder, while the manual method comprises cutting paper with a cutting tool, for example, a pair of scissors, paper trimmer, or blade.

If you choose to go the manual process and use scissors or a blade, you'll need a ruler and pencil to measure the paper. Ensure you use a cutting mat to guard yourself against the surface blade. On the other hand, if you will be using a paper trimmer, you'll have the option to let go of these extra supplies. Choose a width you want for your paper strips and measure them using your paper trimmer or ruler. Using a paper trimmer will deliver strips a lot quicker than with a pair of scissors or a blade.

A shredder might create strips for you rapidly yet won't have the smooth edges you'll need for your preferred paper quilling design. This technique may likewise not deliver to you the appropriate width you want. Buying a shredder for paper quilling can be very costly.

Using a shredder to get paper strips is not advisable. A shredder is not a trusted process for delivering consistent strips and high-quality strips to work within your quilling strips.

What Type of Paper Should I Use for Paper Quilling?

Pre-cut strips will always come in an acid-free paper of the right weight. If you want to cut your paper strips, you should begin with paper that weighs 120 grams per square meter. This is because it is recommended for creating shapes and rolling.

In any case, you can use any size shape from 80 to 160 grams per square meter for paper quilling. Printer paper (normally around 80 grams square meter) is by and large not sufficiently thick, but instead, you should check out other paper weight to know what you want.

Quilling Needle

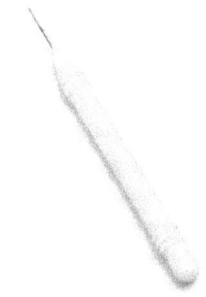

The needle tool is perhaps the most widely used quilling tool by beginner and professional quillers.

With a quilling needle, you can make little centers in scrolls and rolls, which gives way to a more appealing quilling paper design. The 4" elastic handle makes the quiller feel comfortable when rolling quilling paper.

Craft Knife

A craft knife is an essential tool for every paper quiller, but most people do not see its effectiveness. A craft knife is a tool that has a pointed handle. It also features a replaceable blade at two edges and one inch long.

There are different craft knives, including precision cutter, utility knife, art scalpel, and pen cutter.

The different type of craft knife is based on the blade's size, blade type fixed or replaceable blades, and its type of handle design.

Little and built-in blades always seen in precision cutters are used for detail work. The other traditional utility knife, such as a pen cutter, is ideal for all cutting purposes. Also, retractable knives that feature large blades are great for cutting thick materials.

Craft Knife Handle

Crafting knife handle plays a significant role in how your craft knife works. Is the craft knife made to fit easily in your grasp and make the tool easy to hold? All these questions need to be asked before going to purchase your craft knife.

A craft knife that is difficult to hold will not make you feel comfortable or will weaken your hand. Another factor to consider before purchasing your craft knife is the durability feature. Your craft knife handle should be able to last for long periods before rusting.

Craft Glue

Craft glue is any water-based adhesive that can be utilized for making art designs, like your favorite paper quilling design or school projects. Craft glue can be classified into any fast-drying liquid substance. Generally, craft glues are cleaned up using water and soap, and they are not harmful to the human skin. This is why it is perfect for both kids and adults during paper quilling projects.

Craft glues can be purchased in solid or liquid forms, and they are also used to attach materials such as wood, plastic, fabric, and paper. Furthermore, metal glue is used to fix or make jewelry. Other types of metal can join metal to paper for fixing and beautifying furniture and designing artwork.

Cutting Mat

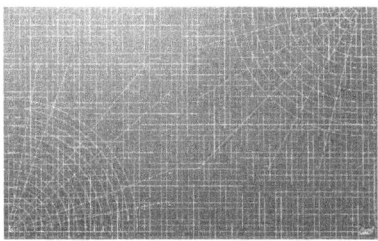

A cutting mat is a surface on which you cut texture using a rotary cutter. Cutting mats are used to guard a surface against the sharp blade edge of the rotary cutter. It is also helpful as it prevents the rotary cutter's blade from losing its sharpness.

Regularly, cutting mats usually have a measured grid printed on their surface to straighten their measured fabric. You can purchase cutting mats as hard-surface, which are not flexible and don't hold any imprints from the rotary cutter's blade.

A cutting mat ensures your work surface doesn't get any marks from the rotary cutter's blade. It likewise increases the life of the blade by making it much sharper.

Numerous cutting mats also have rulers or grid lines, which helps you measure as you carry on cutting your paper strips. When you become acclimated to using sewing tools, you will be ready to choose if you like the mat's different rulers or measuring guides.

Scissors

Scissors are a little cutting tool with two sharp edges. Also, scissors are used for cutting things like paper and fabric. In order to get the perfect paper size, most quillers use scissors. It is a very delicate cutting tool that should be used with caution or else you will ruin your design.

Tweezers

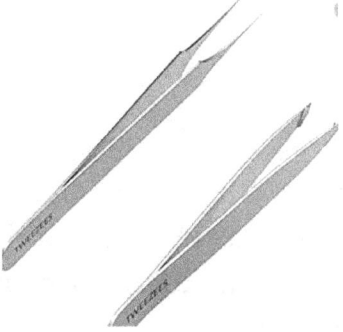

Tweezers are small tools used for picking up objects or items that are so small to be handled by the human fingers. Tweezers are gotten from pincers, scissors-like pliers, or tongs.

Most people often use tweezers essentially for projects such as picking hair from the face or eyebrows. Other essential uses for tweezers are as a tool to pick up little items, including surface-mount, electronic parts, little mechanical parts, and pieces of paper.

Ruler

A ruler is a long level bit of wood, metal, or plastic with straight edges set apart in centimeters or inches. Rulers are majorly used to measure items and to draw straight lines. Paper quillers use rulers to measure the size of their paper quilling project.

Without using a ruler in your paper quilling project, you may not get the near-perfect design you are searching for.

Circular Ruler

The circular rular is used to create perfectly measured bends and circles. Some paper quilling design project requires you to use circular ruler to measure and draw perfect circles carefully.

Sealers

Spray sealants are purchased in an aerosol can, which permits a small sealant spray. Spray sealants are used to seal paper quilling designs to last for long periods. A perfectly sprayed paper quilling design can remain fresh for a long time, even in harsh weather conditions.

How to use sealers

- Endeavor to adhere to the instructions and directions stated by the brand. You will also need to go to a ventilated place and cover the region (for example, table or floor) with a drop material or paper.
- Ensure the paper make is spotless and free from any dust or dirt. In fact, shake the can and afterward hold it 12-14 inches from the design

area. In long smooth strokes, spray the sealant on the top of your paper design and allow it to dry. If the paper design or project has different sides or angles, you should go over the process once more.

Benefits of using sealers

- Spray sealant is lightweight, making it ideal for fragile paper arts, like tissue paper, paper cutting art, large pieces, and paper quilling.
- The spray sealant permits you to seal more little crevices where a brush can't enter.
- Spray sealant also dries fast yet is subject to the number of layers used or the art's size.
- Spray sealant permits layering of sealant and stays flexible.

- The spray sealant is perfect for large pieces since it covers enormous spaces in a short period.

Cutting Paper Quilling Strips

Setting your paper quilling strips has consistently remained an issue for most quillers since they began designing papercrafts. Although there may be kits for paper strips, you may want to consider cutting your own paper quilling strips if you don't want to spend money on it.

In this section, we have compiled the ways you can cut your paper quilling strips in less than 5 minutes:

STEP 1 - Supplies

- Pasta machine with linguini cutter
- Pencil
- Ruler
- Scissors
- A4 piece of paper

The first step is to get your materials and supplies ready. If you have your supplies ready, then it is just a matter of time before you successfully cut your own paper quilling strips. It is always advisable to thoroughly clean your pasta machine once you are done cutting your paper.

Meanwhile, if you cannot get a pasta machine, you can try this method using a paper shredder.

STEP 2: Measure

The most important thing you need to do here is to measure the length of your pasta machine's cutter or paper shredder using a ruler.

Most measurements with a ruler are always around 14,5 cm (5.7"); however, other pasta machines can be different from the figure listed above.

Once you can get the right measurement, simply measure the size on your piece of paper, beginning from the extended side, and sketch a line. If you do this, you will have 2 different parts.

Lastly, cut the paper into two after getting your line.

STEP 3: Create Your Strips

This is where you will create your paper strips for your paper quilling project.

Pick up the largest piece of paper and cautiously insert its short part in the pasta machine while you roll it. Ensure you keep the longest part of the paper entirely corresponding to the side of the machine.

As the rolling process is ongoing, you'll begin seeing your paper strips emerging from the lower part of the pasta machine.

Once the large piece of paper is done, insert the little piece of paper in the cuter as well. Most quilling professionals suggest that you position the piece of paper on the side and be cautious to keep it firm and parallel to the pasta machine.

When the entire process has been completed, your paper strips will be in the region of 0,7cm (0.27") thick. However, the size listed here varies depending on the pasta machine cutter you are using.

STEP 4: Tips and Tricks

At this point, you have successfully cut your own paper strips. Meanwhile, that is not all as there are other couple of things you should be aware of:

- If, for certain reasons, at least two strips are not entirely separated, don't attempt to detach them with your fingers. This is because they are likely to break if you try it.
- You need to cut them with scissors while trying too precisely to make a completely straight cut.
- The strips that emerge from the sides will presumably be somewhat thinner than the others. Although you can barely see the difference, it is

best not to use them with the others because the coils you make with them will be seen when you round up your work.

Basic Paper Quilling Shapes

Paper quilling is a fun way to make beautiful artworks with paper strips. You can easily design any of your favorite paper quilling projects in a short period.

Also, paper quilling comes in different shapes, especially when designing a paper quilling project. Some of the common paper quilling shapes include teardrop, open and closed coils, quilled marquis, and so much more.

Learn the process of making the common and basic paper quilling shapes for your paper quilling project.

1. Open and Closed Coils

Open and closed coils are simply circles made for designing your paper quilling projects. Look below to see the step by step guide on how to make an open and closed coil:

- Start by inserting a strip of quilling paper in the quilling tool slot. Endeavor to get the end of the paper and slot to be as straight as possible. To ensure this is possible, you can use a slotted tool. This is because it will give a small crimp in the middle of your coil.

- The second step is to roll the slotted tool using your functional hand either away from your body or close to it (it all depends on which one makes you feel comfortable). Lastly, hold the strip of paper with your non-functional or non-dominant hand.
- Thirdly, to create a closed coil, apply a little amount of glue close to the strip's end and roll it. Once you take it off from the tool, ensure it does not increase.

- To create an open coil, remove the coil from the tool and leave the coil to increase. When it has increased, simply add a portion of glue and press the strip to cover it.

2. Quilled Teardrop

A quilled teardrop is another common quilling paper shape used by most crafters in their paper quilling project. Check below for the steps to make a quilled teardrop:

- Position an open coil in the middle of your forefinger and thumb of your non-functional hand. Then organize the inner coils and keep them as you would like.

- Using your functional hand, simply pinch the paper to the area you want to form the teardrop shape.

Quilled Teardrop also comes in different forms depending on your preference and what you want to fit perfectly with your paper quilling project.

Here are two different types of quilled Teardrop:

- To create the type of quilled teardrop shape made available here, simply press the shape all over your quilling tool and leave it to get a certain curved shape. This makes you make a paisley shape.
- The second type is to marginally curve the teardrop around your thumb while you are shaping it. This way, you can easily make a subtle shift in shape without tampering with the middle coils. To beautify this change, you can easily cover the teardrop around any cylindrical object or your quilling tool.

3. Quilled Tulip Shape

This step is much easier than the other steps listed above. To make a quilled tulip shape, start by rolling a marquis. Then twist the shape onto its other side and pinch the middle high point using your fingers.

4. **Quilled Marquis**

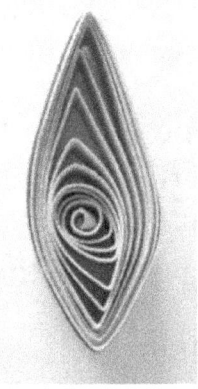

Quilled marquis shape is first created by making a teardrop shape. Once done with creating the teardrop shape, you should pinch it towards the edge's other side.

The amount of coil determines the end of the marquis shape pressed where you positioned the middle of the coil.

5. Quilled Slug Shape

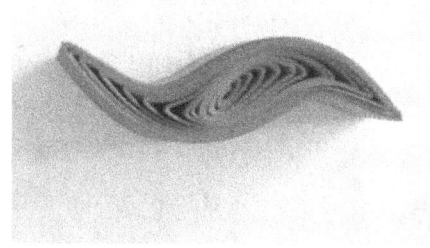

Before creating a quilled slug shape, you need to start by creating a quilled marquis shape. The steps to create a quilled marquis shape are outlined above.

The quilled slug shape is done by either wrapping a quilling tool or covering one end of your fingertip. Afterward, carry out the same process for the other side. However, it needs to be in the other direction.

6. Quilled Rectangle

Making quilled rectangular and square shapes are almost done the same way. However, the slight difference between the two is when the marquis shape is rotated before pinching extra angles.

You can rotate it marginally before pinching and opening the shape to show the ideal and right rectangle size.

On the other hand, you can also make a quadrilateral shape by creating your four edges at an unequal interval. The quadrilateral shaped rectangle is done mostly when crafters make quilled paper mosaics.

7. Quilled Diamond or Square

To create a quilled square or diamond shape, you have to make a basic marquis shape first. When the shaping has been completed, simply rotate the marquis 90 degrees and further pinch the two sides once more.

Once done, the result will be a diamond shape. Meanwhile, if you decide to make a quilt square shape, slowly open the shape between your fingers.

8. **Quilled Triangle**

You can create a quilled triangle shape by first making a teardrop shape. Once you have gotten your teardrop shape, you can either use the tabletop or pinch two extra angles with your fingers.

Triangle shaped paper quilling design can also be done so that it looks like a shark fin. This is easily completed by pressing in both triangle sides and allowing the last side to remain level.

9. Quilled Semi-Circle

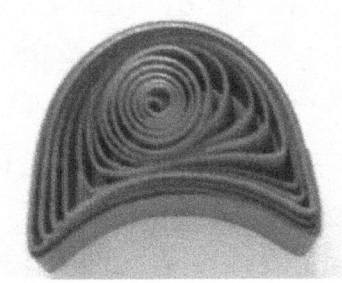

A quilled shaped semi-circle is done by using an open coil and pinching two corners. The quilled semi-circle shape can also be created by pressing an open coil on a hard surface such as a tabletop and inserting your fingers downwards. While doing this, ensure you are careful so that you won't make any mistakes.

10. **Quilled Arrow**

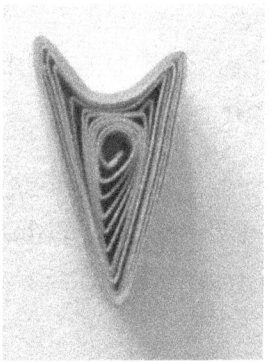

As you have with other common shapes, a quilled arrow shape is created by first making a teardrop. Simply drag down the middle in the direction of the bottom and use your fingers to hold it.

Furthermore, use the longer part of the slotted needle and press down into the bottom. Remove your fingers from the needle and level the curve using your fingers.

11. **Quilled Arrowhead**

Create a teardrop shape first before proceeding to make a quilled arrowhead shape. When completed, hold the pointed edge in your non-functional hand and pinch the bottom edge into a firm point.

Without removing your hand from the pointed edge, slide your fingers to reach the fingers of your other hand to form the slide angles.

12. Quilled Pentagon

To create a quilled pentagon shape, you need to make a long quilled semi-circle shape. Then proceed to pinch the middle of the even side similarly when creating the tulip shape as listed above.

Keep the high point in the middle and square off the base with two even pinches on two sides.

13. Quilled Star

When done creating your quilled pentagon, you can choose to change it to a quilled star. To do this, you need to press in on every even surface using a quilling tool or your fingers and proceed to change every angle to form peaks.

See below for a run down of extra basic shapes some of which will be referred to throughout the course of this book.

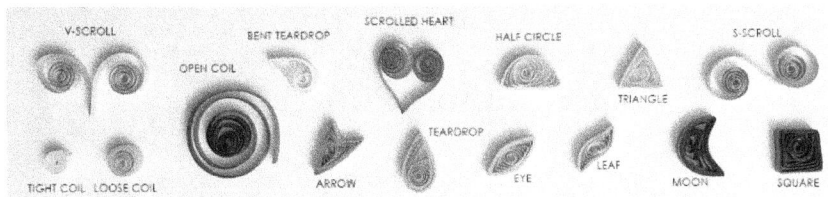

Chapter 5

Paper Quilling Project Ideas

As we all know, paper quilling entails using thin paper strips to shape and join shapes to form a paper design. Don't be bothered because paper quilling is not a costly craft. In fact, you will enjoy the art to the extent of turning it into your hobby.

All you need to get started with any paper quilling project idea is ideally a paper and glue. Although you will need other materials when designing paper crafts, the most important is paper and glue.

Once you have gotten your materials ready, the next thing is to look for a suitable and easy friendly paper quilling pattern or idea to get started. There are 20 beginner and step-by-step paper quilling patterns and project ideas you can try out in the below list.

Photo Frame

Are you in search of a cheap but attractive gift to present to your close friend or family member? The paper quilled photo frame may be the perfect gift that will get your friend or family member excited.

The paper quilled photo frame is made by gluing quilled flowers on all edges of a beautiful frame. So what do you need to make a beautiful paper quilled photo frame?

Materials

- Quilling paper
- Foam board
- Ruler and pencil
- Beads
- Durable and sturdy adhesive glue/craft glue
- X-acto scissors and knife

Steps

1. First of all, take a proper and accurate measurement of your photo frame size. Using your scissors, cut out 2 pieces of foam board and include additional 2 inches on the photo frame size's length and width.
2. Proceed to draw a 1-inch border on the edge of a single piece and draw an upside-down arch shape on the second piece's upper central area. Cut out the piece that resides within the border

and complete it by cutting out the arch shape very carefully.
3. Allow the frame to lie on a smooth surface before taking a measurement and cutting 2 foam board pieces. The cut pieces will serve as the lower area and the sides of the foam. Use your glue to join the pieces in their respective places. The upper part of the frame should not be closed. This is because you would have to place the photo inside the frame once you are done.
4. Subsequently, cut out a pattern from the foam board that looks like a tie. Then cut half along the upper 1.5 cm of the stand and corner it. Use your glue to join the rear side of the frame, and glue the 1.5 cm area of the stand on the rear area diagonally by allowing the edge to match with the edge of the frame.

5. Arrange your paper strips for the quilling process to begin. You can use light colors for the green leaves and flowers. Additionally, you can also use bright and colored paper strips to create a teardrop shape. Create as much as you will need.
6. Put a scrap paper beneath the frame before you begin the paper quilling process on the frame. You can take up a craft or white glue and join the quilled papers.

7. Begin gluing the quilled papers from the edge of the frame. Some people usually use 6 teardrop patterns for every flower. If you like, you can include additional petals.

8. Lastly, Make extra paper quilling flowers on all edges of the frame. Do not try to be too clever by using colors that don't match. You should also glue the green leaves in the middle of the flowers.

Easy Fashionable Quilled Angel

The easy and fashionable quilled angel is a perfect quilling design for kids and adults. Within 15 minutes, you can easily create a beautiful, fashionable quilled angel.

The essence of the easy fashionable quilled angles is to beautify a Christmas tree.

Materials

- White glue
- 5mm quilling paper (White, yellow, and pink colors)
- Rolling pen
- Scissors

Steps

1. Using your rolling pen, roll out a piece of white quilling paper in a round shape format.
2. The next step is to create the wings of the quilling angel. You can do this by curling a piece of the white quilling paper to form a wing and gluing it with your white glue. Then twisting another piece of yellow quilling paper and using white glue to join it as well. When you have completed the yellow and white quilling paper, you can attach them with white glue.

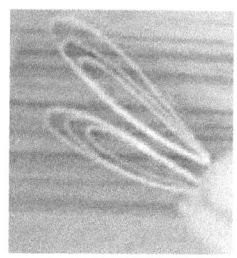

3. Create the tail of the quilling angel. The tails are mostly done by twisting two white quill pieces in a wing form before using white glue. Do the same thing for your yellow quilling paper and attach them. Ensure you place the yellow paper in the center and two white paper pieces on the left and right hand-sides differently.
4. Round up the quilling angel. To complete your paper quilling design, simply roll a piece of pink quilling paper and form it into a heart. Then use white glue to attach the quilling angel's head, tail, pink heart, and wings.

Teardrop Vase

Do you want to beautify the looks of your vase? Well, you can easily do that by making a paper quilled teardrop vase. The design can be achieved with different but beautiful colors.

The paper quilled teardrop vase is a perfect way for beginners to start and engage in their first paper quilling project.

Materials

- Glue – The type of glue needed should be able to glue paper to a ceramic surface.
- Vase – A simple bud shaped ceramic vase would work just fine for this process.
- Quilling needle tool

- Quilling slotted tool
- Paper strips – The paper strips gotten should be in different colors.
- Quilling board – The quilling board is an optional material needed for designing your paper quilled teardrop vase. This material is mainly used to ensure the teardrop vase is made with accurate size.

Steps

1. Roll the paper strips

Beginning with the less bright paper color, place the edge of one paper strip in the quilling slotted tool.

It is important to turn the slotted tool while still having a grip on the paper strip. This will make the paper strip attach to the metal rod. Also, try to make the smooth side of the paper strips stay on the exterior side.

While turning the slotted tool, endeavor to keep the spiral on your finger to hold it from losing its tight state.

If you have successfully created the entire paper strip in a coil, proceed to place the coil in a circle on your quilling board (if you have one), and allow it open to cover the hole.

For people without a quilling board, you can use a ruler, but you need to be cautious while the coil is getting loosed. Still, on the paper strips step, pour a little amount of glue at the edge of the paper strip and on it to make the coil remain in its current state. A quilling needle will work perfectly to ensure the glue is applied without mistake.

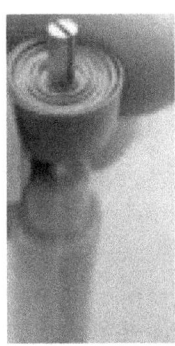

2. Create the Teardrops

Take each coil you have created and form them into a teardrop shape. Do not worry because this step is easy. What you need to carry out is to slowly press half of the coil in the middle of your thumb and finger. You can also pinch an edge to create a sharp fold.

The decision to create a teardrop size lies within you. Once done, you will have to include the teardrops in the vase.

3. Add Teardrops into Vase

Before rounding up your quilling project, you need to create several quilled teardrops. When done, use your glue to attach them to your vase, beginning from the bottom.

Do not use too much glue because you could end up ruining your project. Instead, put a little amount of glue to the back and hold the teardrop on the vase surface. Within 10 minutes or more, the glue should stick to the vase surface.

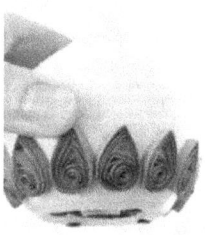

On completion of one row, you can go through the same steps again, but you have to use different colors this time. Create up to 4 or 5 rows using the same steps as mentioned earlier, and you will have your easy and fashionable quilled vase.

Quilled Easter Egg Design

As Easter approaches, you will find different beautiful designs all-around your surroundings. The quilled Easter egg craft is a fun project perfect for both kids and adults during Easter celebrations.

It is also an easy quilling project that will set you on your way to becoming an expert.

Materials

- 5 mm quilling strips (yellow, white, three different shades of green, red).
- Quilling needle or toothpick
- Red and black marker

- PVA glue

Steps

1. Begin by making the leaves utilizing the green strips. Start with a teardrop shape and afterward change it to get the various leaves by squeezing the closures.

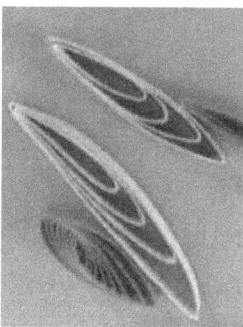

2. Next are the flowers. Use the red strips to make free coils and afterward make folds inside each loop. Make numerous flowers in various sizes.

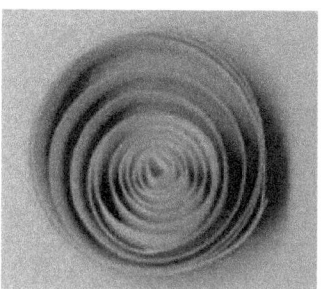 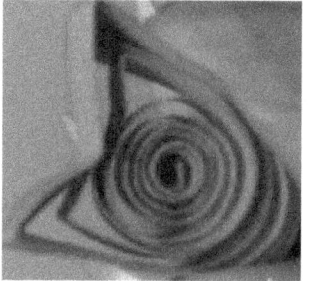

3. Let's proceed to the rabbit. Make a tight coil with three white strips for the rabbit's face. For the ears, make teardrop shapes and squeeze them.

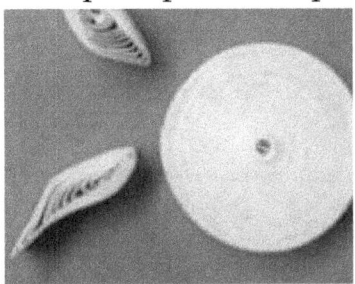

4. For the structure, you should get tight loops in yellow, each made with a full strip.

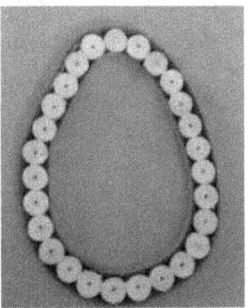

5. Once all the coils are ready, design them in an egg shape and glue them. Leave them to dry for some time. When dry, fold a green strip on top of it and within it.

6. Collect all the parts together. Start with the rabbit by putting it at the base of the egg.
7. Arrange the leaves around the rabbit, and fix the flowers to the branches.
8. Use hued markers – red for the rabbit's ears and dark for facial highlights.

Fall Tree

Fall is perhaps the most wonderful period of the year, and it becomes evident when the leaves begin evolving to another color. Find out the various phases of designing a beautiful paper quilled fall tree.

Materials

- Quilling paper strips – 5mm (Red, Yellow, Orange, Brown Colors)
- Scissors
- Glue
- White cardstock 6 x 12 inches
- Slotted quilling tool

Steps

1. Choose between 3 or 4 fall colored quilling strips. With a 10-inch long quilling strip, coil the whole strip while using your slotted quilling tool.
2. Remove the coiled strip from the slotted quilling tool and leave the coil to release up a bit. Use the glue to cover the open edge to make sure the free coil shape is tightened.
3. Use your fingers to press any sides of the free coil set in the former steps to make a teardrop shape.
4. Subsequently, press the other side of the coil's formerly squeezed side to make an eye shape. Use the glue to cover the open edge of the strip to cover the shape.

5. Likewise, make more important eye shapes with fall colored quilling strips. It will act as the leaves.

6. Pick up the brown colored quilling strips and cut them into your preferred size. With the slotted tool, coil around 1 or 1.5 inches of the strip from a single end of your choice.
7. Equally, get ready 6 to 8 additional strips as done in the former steps.

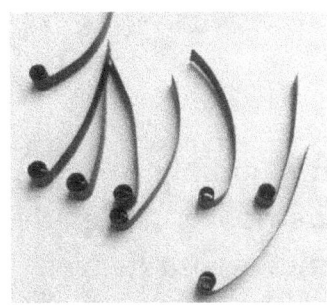

8. Fold a small part of white cardstock paper halfway to create a card. Also, use the glue to attach the strips to the paper.
9. Pick up the eye shapes and begin to attach them over the trunk area.
10. When attaching the leaf shapes, try to stay with an attractive mix.
11. Once done, leave the glue to dry.

Hedgehog

When we discuss quilling, we mean creating coils with long thin paper strips; however, there's another quilling type– one identified with hedgehogs. It is the situation where a youthful hedgehog's spines drop out to clear a path for grown-up spines. How about we blend the two in with an adorable little quilled hedgehog design?

Look below for the materials and step by step guide.

Materials

- Craft paperwhite, pink and dim
- Craft glue
- Scissors
- Black sharpie
- Slotted quilling tool
- Quilling paper strips

Steps

1. Create the base for the hedgehog's body and head. You can do this by using a dark brown colored 20" strip for the body and a light brown

colored 18" strip for the head. Make free coils with the two strips.

2. Press one end of the light brown colored coil to make a sharp edge.

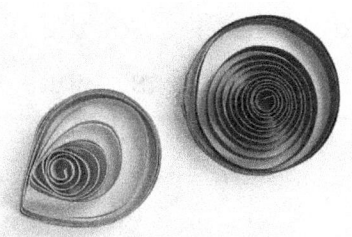

3. Do a similar thing at two different coil edges, to create two more sharp ends, making an uneven triangle shape.

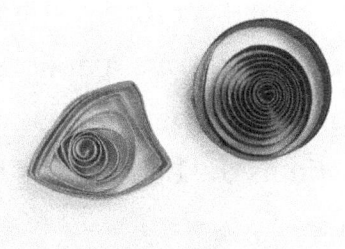

4. Pick up light-colored brown strips of 2" and make extra little triangle shapes. These will be the

spikes of the hedgehog. Create more depending on your needs.

5. Create other body areas of the hedgehog. You can do this by using 3 black quilling pieces of 4" to make tight coils. Two of the black quilling strips will serve as the legs, while the last strip will serve as the hedgehog's nose.

6. Since the hedgehog we are designing is two dimensional, we'll require just a single eye. Make a circle from white art paper and a half-smile shape from pink art paper. Ensure the sizes are in the same ratio as the hedgehog's head and body.

7. Now is the time to assemble everything. Select a sheet of art paper in black color and use your glue to attach the body and quilled head coils made after the initial three stages.

8. With caution, cut the art paper around the hedgehog's head and body. Then glue the three-sided spikes on top of the hedgehog's body, beginning from the center on the way to the back.

9. Finally, stick on the mouth and eye on the hedgehog's head. Place the legs and nose in the suitable areas and allow the hedgehog to dry.

Bats

We all know bats are not attractive and loveable, but with this paper quilling project, they will look charming and adorable. Bats are beautiful designs to add to your extra Halloween stylistic decorations. Let's go on a ride to achieving a paper quilling bat.

Materials

- Art paperwhite, grey, and pink
- Quilling paper strips
- Scissors
- Art glue
- Black sharpie
- Slotted quilling tool

Steps

1. Pick up a 20-inch long quilling strip and coil the entire strip with the slotted quilling tool. Remove the coil from the quilling tool and leave the coil to release up. When you are happy with the coil size, use the glue to cover the coil's open edge.
2. Also, glue the free coil on a black color art paper.
3. Cautiously cut the art paper all around the coils' external end.
4. Pick up a 10-inch long quilling strip and make a free coil design.
5. Use your fingers and press any side of the free coil to create a teardrop shape.

6. Additionally, press the other two opposite sides of the teardrop (this will create a three-sided shape).
7. Press and fold in the center area of any two squeezed sides of the three-sided shape. Likewise, make additional designs. The first 2 will serve as the bat wings; you should make 2 additional shapes for the wing.

8. Use 5 inches quilling strip and create a three-sided shape. Additionally, make an extra one. It will be for the bat ears.

9. Make use of a 5-inch quilling strip to form 2 focal point shapes, 4-inch quilling strips to make 2 focal point shapes, and 2-inch quilling strip to make 2 free coils.
10. Place the already arranged items on a level surface to see the bat design.
11. Use your glue to attach the prepared parts individually.
12. Cut out the mouth, teeth, and eyes of the bat. You can use white art paper to remove the teeth and the eyes. With a black sharpie, draw or sketch the eyeballs and use a pink art paper for the mouth area.
13. Glue the finished parts on the large free coil design. Give the glue enough time to dry.

Wreath Ornament

The most known way to realize that the Christmas season is here is to see attractive Christmas designs on people's main doors. You can design a little quilled wreath ornament for your apartment or someone else.

Also, you can likewise design a smaller one for Christmas cards or presents. It is a design suitable for beginners and all ages.

Materials

- Quilling Tools
- Quilling Strips in light green and red, and dark green
- Art Glue

Steps

1. Begin by using the dark green quilling strips. Create covered coils in a petal shape by using the art glue. You'll require about 15 petal shapes for one small wreath.

2. When you have sufficient dark green petals, organize them in a circle. Organize them initially on a flat piece of paper to perceive how they will likely work. Use glue to attach the petals. Allow it to dry and hold the wreath.

3. Make extra small petal shapes out of the light green quilling strips. Furthermore, create tightly covered coils from the red strips.

Flower Garden

Whenever you design a flower, it is normal that the change will reflect in a flower garden, with butterflies, ladybugs, etc.

The flower garden quilling craft is a paper quilling art you will enjoy showing on your wall. It is also a paper design that will light up your home and brighten your mood.

Materials

- Quilling strips (yellow, red, dark green, pink, white, brown colored and light green)
- Thick cardstock or painting canvas
- Scissors

- Quilling tool
- Watercolor paints (green, brown, and blue)
- Craft Glue

Steps

1. Begin with the background for the proposed wall art. You can use a painting canvas or go for truly thick cardstock, which you would then attach to cardboard.
2. Use blue watercolor for the top part of the canvas and green for the bottom part. Allow the paint to wash over to present a refined effect.

3. Also, use the light green quilling paper to make leaf stems and shapes. Organize them equally

through the base side of the canvas, yet make them of various sizes.
4. Leave a little space in the middle where the flowers can reside.
5. Let's use a sunflower, for example. Create a base (a wide circle from the green paper). Make yellow petal shapes and attach them to the base, making sure there are sufficient petals to be shared.
6. To create the middle, you will have to use fringed strips. Use a solid bulldog clip to hold the strip while you cut to make fringes with your sharp scissors.

You need some fringed strips for the middle. Explore with a quilling tool to make thick coils with the fringed strips, adding extra strips to raise the length.

The completed coil should fit comfortably in the middle of the yellow flower. When you get the correct size, stop and glue the edges. Once dried, cushion out the fringes somewhat and cut off lost edges. Also, glue it into the middle of the sunflower.

7. Proceeding to the pink flowers, which are genuinely easy to design, create petal shapes out of pink paper and glue them. Once dry, place them in a suitable spot.
8. Create a twofold circle using white paper inside and pink outwardly. Make 6-7 of such circles, attach them at the base, and close with pink paper. For the top wings, which are smaller, press the whole wing together and squeeze the edges.
9. To design a butterfly's body, make two shapes with pink paper. Correct the vault's base into the base of the stick and stone. When dry, gather the butterfly by placing the wings around it.

Watermelon Jewelry

Regardless of whether you are enjoying your summer at an extraordinary camp, at the seashore, or on vacation somewhere else, this quilled watermelon jewelry will always have its unique looks.

Suitable for kids and adults, simply create the paper quilled watermelon jewelry at your leisure time.

Materials

- Glue
- Quilling needle
- Quilling strips (white, red, light green, and dark green shade of 5mm)
- Pendant holder

- Black marker

Steps

1. Design a tight coil with the 15 quilling strips of red color.
2. Pick up double white-colored quilling strips and fold them over the red tight coil. At that point, also pick up two light green colored quilling strips and go through the same process but not the white color.
3. Keep on with the same procedures for the dark green colored strips but don't forget that while folding it over the light green color, after one round of wrapping, place a pendant holder through the strip and keep on wrapping. Each time you arrive at the pendant holder, put the quilling strip through it and not any other way. Once done, glue the paper's end.

4. With a black marker, draw little specks everywhere on the red tight coil.

Flower Cake

Whenever you need to make a cake for a unique event, you can design it with a paper quilled flowers cake. It works just fine in decorating and beautifying your cake.

Let's get right into the materials needed and how to make a paper quilled flowers cake

Materials

- Glue stick
- Yellow paper
- White printer paper
- Scissors or paper shaper

Steps

1. To achieve a fringed middle, cut a little yellow cardstock (1.5 cm X 3 cm) and fringe the end. Move it up and close it using glue.
2. To achieve the flower petals, cut 1/4" of printer paper strips.
3. Move up the strip into a tight coil, allow it to unroll a piece, and secure it using glue.

4. Using two fingers, squeeze the round coil at the closures, so the shape turns out to be all the more a diamond.
5. Keep on making the diamond shapes until you are sure you have sufficient petals.
6. For a twofold diamond petal, create two jewel coils and crunch them together, ensuring their safety by folding another paper strip over the two pieces' external edge and attaching them with glue.

7. Finally, glue all your completed petals around the fringed middle part.

Snowflakes

It is never too soon to begin contemplating designing Christmas crafts. You can call on your kids to make these exquisite quilled snowflakes to beautify your Christmas tree.

They are very attractive that you can use them as cheap presents for your friends and family members. Virtually everybody will cherish a gift that you made with your hands, and it makes the gift to carry more significance.

Materials

- Scissors
- Pencil
- Thin ruler
- Glue
- Quilling slotted tool
- White sheet of paper
- Plastic sheet paper
- Geometric compass
- Paper quilling strips (5mm wide and 54cm long of White and Blue color)

Steps

1. First of all, know how long the strips are for your quilled snowflakes.
2. With a compass, draw a 5 cm circle on the white sheet. This will serve as the bottom area.
3. Subsequently, partition the circle into 6 equivalent parts and draw your plan.

4. For the initial fold– Tight Coil, move up a strip around an opened slotted too. Paste your glue to the end.

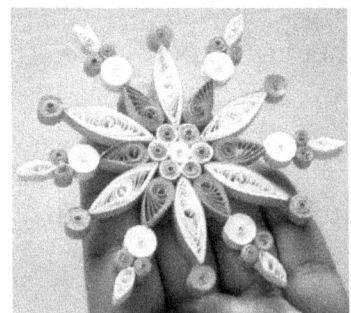

5. For the other fold, which is teardrop, roll a strip around a slotted tool. Carefully remove it from the slotted tool, allow it to extend more than two fingers. You're your other hand, slowly squeeze one end to create a leaf or a teardrop. Also, glue the end.
6. The last fold, which is the eye or the marquis, move up a strip around a slotted tool firmly. Slowly remove it from the slotted tool, allow it to extend between two fingers. Using your two hands, squeeze the two ends to create an eye like design and glue the edges.
7. To create the snowflakes, below are the materials needed:
    - 6 full-length marquis in white
    - 6 full-length tears in blue
    - 1 half-length tight coil in white
    - 6 half-length tight coils in blue
    - 6 quarter-length marquis in white
    - 6 full-length tight coils in white
    - 18 quarter-length tight coils in blue

9. At this point, you should be prepared to gather. Put the drawing beneath an OHP sheet and begin gathering each piece from the middle. Start with the white half-close coil. Glue the blue quarter coils around it. At that point, attach the teardrop.

Furthermore, use the white marquis in the middle of the tears and smaller than normal marquis to round up.

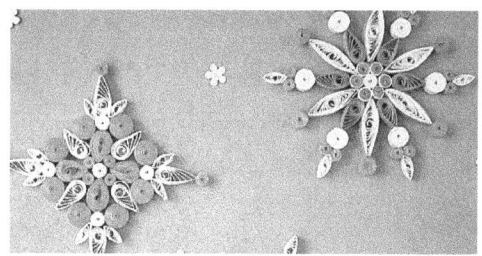

10. Allow it to dry totally so that each fold is adhered solidly to the one close to it. You could cover it with a spray clear varnish if you want.

Flower Basket

This quilled flower basket has a pleasant scent that can attract people around. This is why the paper quilling flower basket is one of the most crafted designs for households. Once done, it can be hung on your wall.

Materials

- White stationery paper
- Scissors
- Art glue
- Quilling paper strips
- Slotted quilling tool

Steps

1. Pick up a 10 inches quilling strip and coil the whole piece with the slotted quilling tool.
2. Remove the coiled strip out of the slotting tool cautiously.
3. Leave the coil to free up a piece without anyone touching it.
4. Squeeze any one side of the free coil to create a teardrop shape. Then attach the open edge of the strip to cover the shape.
5. Likewise, make additional teardrop shapes. For every flower, you would need about 6 teardrop shapes.

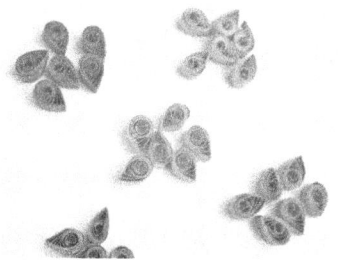

6. Pick up a green-colored quilling strip and make a free coil.
7. Press the other side of the free coil to create an eye shape. Apply the glue to the open end of the strip to cover the shape.
8. Make other eye shapes specifically for the leaves. You can use green-colored strips.
9. Take a yellow colored strip to make semi-free coils; Make 1 for every flower you have designed.

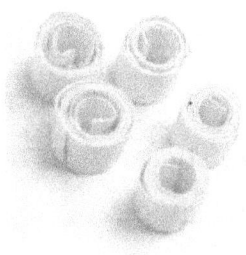

10. Use a brown colored shaded strip to make free coils. The brown-colored free coils will be utilized to make the basket design.

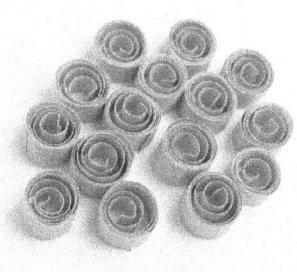

11. Pick up a bit of white fixed paper; assemble the art glue and strips.
12. To make the flower design, attach 1 yellow semi-free coil and glue any 6 teardrop shapes between the coils to finish the flower design.
13. Make the other flower designs; place the flowers adjacent to one another.
14. Using glue, paste the leaf designs in the middle of the flower designs; Use the brown-colored free coils to make the basket.
15. Leave the glue to dry, and you have completed the process.

Paper Quilled Tops

People use paper quilling for creating and designing toys. Kids will be excited with this paper top art, and even adults can get into it as well. You only need to make a round paper coil for the lower part of the top and create a mass of paper to shape the base.

Materials

- Toothpicks
- 1/4" paper strips
- White glue

Steps

1. It is truly significant that the initial strip is firmly onto the toothpick and stuck with glue. It is recommended that you use a wrapping for the initial round onto numerous other toothpicks and providing them with a small time to dry before including the next strips.

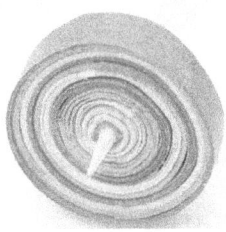

2. Include a little glue to the end of the initial strip and twist the strip around the toothpick, about 1/2" from the tip. Apply extra glue to the strip and attempt to keep the toothpick vertical. In the wake of wrapping the main strip, leave to dry and begin 3 or 4 additional tops.

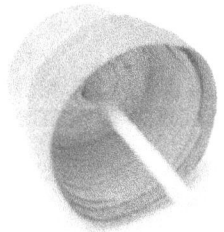

The three tops include:

1. A circle: all columns are covered in the same style. The outcomes are looking extraordinary.
2. A little disc with ventured upsides.
3. A small disc (a couple of rows) with ventured upsides.

Monogram

Several crafters create paper quilled monograms to give as wedding gifts or to decorate their home walls.

You don't need to spend too much money to begin designing paper quilled monogram. All you require is paper, a stick, and a circle object.

In case you're nibbled by the quilling bug, you will need to buy tools, including a quilling pen, brush, and crimper. With enough time, practice, and patience, you will become an expert in making paper quilled monograms.

Materials

- Scissors
- Tweezers
- 1 shadowbox picture frame
- Little paintbrush for glue
- Craft paper slimmer
- Card stock quilling strips your favorite colors
- 1 Paper plate

Steps

1. Print your preferred letter, covered with a light or dark background shade you like on the card stock background.
2. Cut the strips. Pick card stock in different colors you intend to fit into your plan. You can use the paper shaper to cut paper from the card stock that line one-quarter inch wide.

3. Shape the Strips. When you choose the plan within your letter, it's an ideal opportunity to make shapes.

   Pick up a paper strip and wrap it around your quilling tool or toothpick into the shape you like, either moved firmly (for a reduced shape) or freely, depending on your choice.

   Apply a small quantity of glue on the end of the paper strip to hold the shape.

4. Design your letter with paper strips. You can use your favorite technique to paste glue to the bits of paper that will shape your letter frame.

5. Cover the outside of the letter using paper strips

- Glue and put your strips on the design of your letter. Use your fingers to hold the strips tenderly until the glue is tight for the paper strip to stand up all alone.
- Create a crisp fold on a piece of paper and apply glue on each end and cover it on every side. This little strip will cover the corners.
- Apply glue and cover a quarter-inch strip as an anchor elsewhere you have a combined strip of paper. The covering will make the casing firmer.
- Leave the wall of your quilled letter to dry altogether.
6. Start filling in your letter frame. Whenever you have assembled your external frame, fill in the internal parts of your monogram.
    - Follow your plan and glue your strips and shapes into place; use your fingers and tweezers for restricted areas.
    - Leave the completed piece to dry totally for a couple of hours.
7. Utilize your tweezers. Tweezers are a quillers closest companion. They are perhaps the main tools used

for pulling paper shapes of different sizes into little spaces in your monogram design without upsetting the frame.

8. Frame the completed quilled monogram. Once dry, place the piece in your shadowbox outline.

Reindeer

These adorable quilled Christmas reindeer are the perfect hand-made design for your holiday presents this year. It is beginner-friendly, and kids mostly make them.

Materials

- Quilling tool

- Light Brown Beige, Red and Brown Quilling Paper
- Tags
- Googly Eyes

Steps

1. The reindeer works by using many marquis shapes in various sizes, mainly for the antlers. You can use beige and brown paper to create it.
2. Create two sizeable brown petal shapes to serve as the head of the reindeer.
3. Also, create a large tight coil using light brown paper to serve as the face.
4. Finally, use a tight red coil to design the nose and the googly eyes.

Candy Cane

Want to design a paper quilled candy cane for special events? This section specifically focuses on making a paper quilled candy cane.

Materials

- Tags
- Red, Green, and White Quilling Paper
- Quilling Tools

Steps

1. Create free coils in white and red, mainly for the cane.
2. Also, create marquis shapes from the green paper specifically for the leaves.
3. Lastly, connect the white and red coils, on the other hand on the tag, and connect the marquis shapes on the upper part.

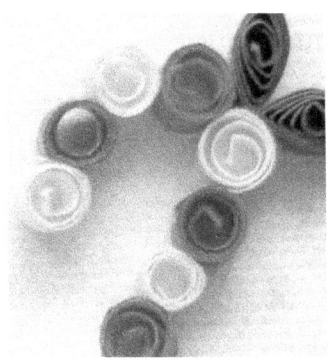

3D Corrugated Flowers

Folded or corrugated cardboard makes art crafts look attractive. A perfect example of corrugated cardboard is the 3D Corrugated Sheet Quilled Flowers. This design is not a difficult one, and both kids and adults can carry out this task.

Materials

- A4 sized corrugated sheet Blue
- A4 sized corrugated sheet Red
- A4 sized corrugated sheet green
- A4 sized corrugated sheet Yellow
- A4 sized corrugated sheet dark
- Scissors
- Lace

- Glass container
- Glue Gun
- Black marker

Steps

1. Pick up the A4 sheets and cut them into 1/2 inch strips.
2. Ensure you cut the A4 sheet along the short edge to get a dazzling zig-zag design contrary to what would be expected on the strip.
3. The benefit of utilizing an A4 sheet is that the length is the equivalent for each strip, and you can cut it as wide as you need the 3D effect to look like.
4. In terms of the petals, roll each strip in a free circular style and paste the end or edge.

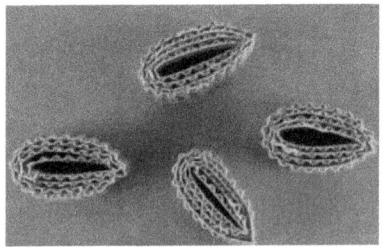

5. When the glue dries, squeeze one end to frame a petal-like shape.
6. The best way to arriving at a decent petal shape is to roll the strip free.
7. For the middle, firmly roll the yellow strip and glue.
8. Organize the petals in a circular way around the middle and glue them. Leave it to dry.
9. Design as many flowers as you want. You will require 6 strips to create one flower.
10. To provide it with a few shading, you can use a beautiful soft petal.
11. Cut the green into leaf sizes
12. Cut a few petal shapes from the folded sheets and glue them to the front.
13. Add a few stems by folding a dark sheet into little lines.

Turkey Design

If you have designed a pie, cranberry sauce, and some other designs for yourself or a family member, you can try out making a paper quilled turkey craft.

You only need two basic quilling shapes and one cut cardboard to make this incredible turkey craft. Let's get right into the materials required.

Materials

- Quilling paper strips (fall colors)
- Black sharpie
- Turkey template
- Scissors
- White cardstock paper
- Slotted quilling tool

- Art glue

Steps

1. Before commencing the paper quilled turkey design, you need to start with canvas. Here's what you should do: Roll a strip of white cardstock paper halfway to create a card. You can also cut and glue a strip of green art paper 1.5 inches wide and glue it beneath the card.
2. Choose the art papers for the turkey and follow the designs from the template on the preferred papers. To cut out the traced designs, use a pair of scissors.
3. Next, use art glue to attach the components to create the body of the paper turkey.

4. Pick up a 10-inch long quilling strip and coil it using the slotted quilling tool. You can also use the coiled strip to create the slotted tool and permit the coil to free up.
5. Pick up the free coil and squeeze any of the sides to create a teardrop shape.
6. Press the other side of the former squeezed side to create a basic eye shape. Then use your glue to attach the open end to cover the shape.
7. You can go through the same method to form additional basic eye shapes.
8. Other from 3 free coils: 2 of the loose coils will serve as the turkey's feet, and the remaining will be in your favorite color.
9. Attach all the card components to create the turkey card.
10. Pick up the orange eye-shaped paper quilled strips and attach the pieces to the paper.
11. Glue the yellow colored paper quilled strips on the second layer and create an arch shape.
12. Furthermore, also glue the third layer and glue the 1 colored free coil underneath the eye-shape.

13. Lastly, glue the paper turkey design on the loose coil and include the orange free coils to create the turkey's feet. Once done, leave the glue to dry.

Shamrock Card

The paper-quilled shamrock card design has everything similar to St. Patrick's Day. It features different colors, with the common one being rainbow. The color green is what is mostly found in the paper quilled shamrock card design.

Materials

- An A6 card
- Glue
- Toilet paper roll

- Strips of rainbow paper
- Scissors
- Toothpick
- Green paper strips

Steps

1. Prepare your rainbow card. This is an optional step, but some people prefer to paint a rainbow on their card or use pens to create a rainbow card.
2. Prepare your toilet paper shamrock pattern. Pick up your toilet paper roll and cut out 4 pieces at least 1cm wide. You should also refold the 4th piece to create a tree-shaped shamrock stem. Once you are done, glue the design.

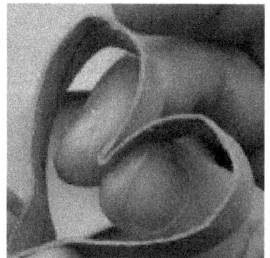

3. Paper quill your shamrock card. Here, you are expected to cut out 1cm piece of different colors and lengths. Use a toothpick and coil the paper

around the shamrock card. Go through the same procedures until you get several green paper quills.

4. Glue it and begin slotting in the paper quills. Use glue to cover the toilet paper roll shamrock and begin slotting your paper quills. Ensure you have an attractive blend of sizes and shades.

3D Snowman Design

It is crucial to share love during the Christmas season, and there is no better way to do so than by creating a paper quill 3D snowman design. If you don't have snow around you, this design is the right choice for you to make.

Materials

- Glue
- Quilling paper (Red, white, blue)
- Red and black marker pens
- Pencil
- Quilling tool

Steps

1. Create the snowman's bottom and make it 3D so that it can stand. To do this, create four firm coils from white paper. Two of the coils will be for the body, while the other two will be for the bases. Also, create two little firm white coils for its head.
2. Proceed to create the blue hat. In this step, you will need a cone. Begin by creating a firm coil using blue quilling paper, using a pointed pencil,

and positioning the point in the middle of the coil.

3. To close the hat, simply place a white paper quilling piece on the edge and create a little firm blue coil and glue it to the hat top.
4. Go through similar methods to create a cone for the snowman's nose using red quilling paper. Create the scarf using red paper and blue strips.
5. Arrange any of the snowmen by organizing a body, base, scarf, red nose, head, and blue hat. Create the eyes using a black marker and the mouth using a red marker.
6. For the snowman's hat, create a firm coil using 5 strips.

7. Lastly, pick up a long red quilling paper pieces and cover it with a quilling tool or pencil. Hold it firmly and remove the beautiful curls.

New Year Quilling Greeting Card

Begin the New Year by presenting a beautiful quilling greeting card. This is a great way to show and spread love to your friends and family members.

The New Year quilling greeting card can be done easily, and kids can even engage in the design.

Materials

- Scissors
- 5mm yellow quilling paper

- Glue
- 5mm red quilling paper
- Tweezers
- Quilling pen
- Quilling models
- Card

Steps

1. Create green and red petals. In this first step, you must cut 5 strips of 5mm green and red quilling papers. Then roll the cut quilling papers using a rolling pen and place them in a 12 cm-sized hole to regulate each of them.

    Glue the tail and hold and place one point using tweezers and press the other side with your fingers to create or design a petal-like shape. Go through similar procedures to create the other petals.

2. Create quilling paper flowers. Plan and arrange card papers before sticking 5 green petals underneath the card. Proceed to stick the other petals on the top of the green flower. Then cut a

little part of 5mm yellow quilling paper and move it in the small bead.

Then place the yellow quilling paper on the flower to create a bud.

3. Include extra ornaments. To create extra ornaments, roll 2 strips of red quilling paper and form them into a small shape. Proceed to stick the ornaments into the other side and cut them.
4. Include quilling paper candles. This is the final step in designing a New Year greeting card. In this step, you need to cut 9 strips of red quilling paper and roll them in 8cm beads one after the other.

Then stick 5 red quilling paper to one side and 4 to the other side. Trim 2 strips of yellow quilling paper and roll all into 8cm bead. Connect one edge using tweezers and press the other edge to shape them.

Place them to the upper part of the candles, and you should be done.

Chapter 6

Resolving Paper Quilling Common Mistakes

Perhaps you were making a paper quilling design, and you made a grave or small mistake. Don't worry because it is common to beginners. Some of the paper quilling mistakes made can even brighten or beautify your paper quilling design.

Besides, you cannot be perfect, so mistakes are bound to happen. Professionals and experts are also not left out with making mistakes. Once you make a mistake while designing a particular paper quilling design, simply take a deep breath and look for possible solutions.

This section details the common paper quilling mistakes made by quillers and the solutions you can follow to correct them.

1. **Excess glue**

One of the common paper quilling mistakes is the application of too much glue. Pouring more glue than needed on your paper quilling design can ruin your hard work and render it useless.

One rule of thumb is to pour lesser glue than needed. This will save you from experiencing any glue problem.

The design is only but a paper and so excess glue is not advisable. In fact, the paper quilling designers who are now professionals often dip a little dot of glue on their paper quilling design.

If you are having difficulties controlling how you pour glue, you are advised to use a needle-nosed bottle.

2. Coils not leveled

Another common paper quilling mistake is the issue of uneven coils. Most people often battle with preventing uneven paper quilling shapes and coils, but there is a way to go about it.

Whenever you need to give your coils a good shape, you have to hold the coil's middle with one hand and pinch the coil with your other hand. As a result, the middle of the coil will stay where it should be, and it won't move to any sides (which can be damaging).

Additionally, if you will like to create even coils all the time, you should consider using a quilling template work board. This will prevent the coils from spreading more than it should.

3. **Uneven dried shapes**

It can be a challenging experience to have uneven dried shapes on your paper quilling patterns. It is also a challenging experience to ensure your entire paper quilling strips are well leveled when they dry on your work board.

In some situations, you might not even know that a part of your shape has come up. The best solution to fixing uneven dried shapes is by using a craft or art knife.

Here's how it works: move the blade along with the two shapes, and you should have your even dried shape. Alternatively, you can also use an even edge before the strips become dried.

4. **Dried glue fingers**

Virtually every paper quilling designer has experienced this issue one way or the other. It is never a nice feeling removing dried glues from fingers.

This is why you should always place a moist towel close to where you are working so that you can easily clean your fingers each time you apply glue.

5. **Wrinkled backs**

The primary cause of wrinkled backgrounds is that the paper is very thin to hold up the glue required for joining the different paper strips.

The most recommended option for preventing wrinkled backgrounds is a thick mat board. Another top to avoid wrinkled backgrounds is to apply small glue. You can choose to apply small dots and not closing the whole strips before mounting.

6. Double thickness strips have a bubble

The double thickness bubble strip is an almost unavoidable mistake. When applying glue, there will be some situations where you will find a gap. These glue gaps will result in a buckled area in your paper quilling strips.

You may not see this mistake until you want to use the strip on your paper quilling design. The best solution to this mistake is by using small scissors to close the bubble.

7. Crooked backgrounds

It would be unfortunate to know that you are done with a paper quilling project and spot a small crooked on its back. But this mistake is a slight one that is probably not your fault, and you can correct it easily.

You can solve this issue by cutting the background small. If the completed work is on a frame, the mistake will not be seen.

Another recommended option to take is to mount the paper quilling once again. Take a craft or art knife and cut around the whole strip. Although it might stay way higher due to the extra backing, it is better than having a crooked quill.

The end... almost!

Hey! We've made it to the final chapter of this book, and I hope you've enjoyed it so far.

If you have not done so yet, I would be incredibly thankful if you could take just a minute to leave a quick review on Amazon

Reviews are not easy to come by, and as an independent author with a little marketing budget, I rely on you, my readers, to leave a short review on Amazon.

Even if it is just a sentence or two!

So if you really enjoyed this book, please...

\>\> Click here to leave a brief review on Amazon.

I truly appreciate your effort to leave your review, as it truly makes a huge difference.

Chapter 7

Paper Quilling Frequently Asked Questions

During your paper quilling journey, there may be one question or the other which may be bothering your mind. It is perfectly normal because you cannot become a professional when designing a paper quilling item for the first time.

Meanwhile, we have rallied around and compiled the most frequently asked questions from several paper quilling designers. Take a look below:

Q – What paper size should I use for quilling?

Ans – The paper size you should use for your quilling design is dependent on the type of design you want to create. However, the most used paper quilling design is carried out using 1/8" (3mm) wide quilling paper.

Furthermore, the 3/8" and 1/4" quilling papers are mainly used for fringed flowers, miniatures, and folded roses.

Q – What kind of paper is used to quill?

Ans – Papers meant for quilling comes in different forms and sizes. However, the paper used to quill is carried out with text weight paper, which is much harder than the regular printer paper. It is also lighter than the typical card stock.

As a matter of fact, card stock is not sufficient for paper quilling because it is likely a curve and not roll

Q – What should I do if my coils do not appear to have a similar size?

Ans – Perhaps you are designing a paper quilling project, and your coils do not appear to have a similar size, even though you started using a similar length strip, and you are bothered about what you should do.

If the above happens to you, simply ensure you apply pressure or force when the rolling process starts. Additionally, you can use a circle template board or circle sizer rule to ensure the coils have the same size.

Q – Why does the slotted tool not open wide when the coil is removed?

Ans – The slotted tool may not open wide when you remove the coil because you may be rolling the strip firmly, which is not supposed to be.

To correct this issue, you need to free up the coil when you apply pressure.

Q – What kind of glue is required for effective paper quilling designs?

Ans – To get the perfect paper quilling design, you need to purchase or obtain water-based glue. Also, ensure that the glue you are using is not too sticky or tacky, as it could ruin your paper quilling design.

Q – How long does it take to become a quilling expert?

Ans – Paper quilling is among those sets of ideas and designs that many people imagine will be easy due to the inexpensive materials and procedures, but that may not be the case for a beginner.

At the initial stage, paper quilling might be a daunting task because you have never been exposed to such mind-blowing designs. However, as time goes on, rolling paper or engaging in paper quilling will start to become as easy as you earlier thought.

Depending on the paper quilling project you are handling, you can either complete it in a few hours or even the next day. It is a great hobby that will boost your creativity level when you are starting new.

Becoming a paper quilling professional is solely dependent on the number of quilling projects at your disposal and the willingness to learn more about the craft.

Q – What is the recommended glue, and how can it be applied?

Ans – Our recommended glue for your paper quilling project is a clear gel adhesive. In comparison with other craft glues, the clear gel adhesive does not grow a surface skin.

Furthermore, this recommended glue does not contain acid and odor like most craft glue. The best way to apply craft glue to your paper quilling project is to dip the tip of the tool you are using and placing it on the surface of your quilling design.

Q – Will my hand feel cramp when designing a paper quill project?

Ans – No. Your hands will never cramp when you are designing your preferred paper quill project. The only way you may experience a cramp on your hands is when you hold a particular tool very firmly for long periods without taking a break.

Let's be real here: most stuff we hold tightly and for a long time will often affect our hands and give us cramp. The perfect solution here is always to be conscious of the grip you have on the paper quilling tool. You can also drip the tools and stretch your fingers and hands once in a while.

Other people choose to tape padding all over the tool's handle for ease of use.

Q – Why is fixative not advisable to coat your completed paper quilling?

Ans – Most people do not like to use fixative because to coat their finished paper quilling design because it affects the design paper's natural look. A few fixatives have the outcome of a shiny and plastic finish.

In most instances, it makes the coil's middle to rise, which is not good for your paper quilling design. For people who create framed paper quilling design, the glass guards it against the harsh weather conditions, especially if it's kept outside.

Q – How can you store quilling paper?

Ans – There is no definite answer to this question because there are many ways you can store quilling paper. The necessary thing to remember about storing quilling paper is to keep it in a dust-free and dry area and not anywhere near direct sunlight.

If you can keep your quilling paper in a dust-free and dry area, it will help the colors stay bright and sharp like you just completed the design.

Q – Can I quill without using a pattern?

Ans – Yes. It is possible to quill paper without a pattern. Basically, there are two kinds of quillers. One is those who use patterns to follow instructions before they paper quill, and the others decide within themselves that they can quill paper without using a pattern.

Most people who use a pattern often make changes during designing a paper quilling project, while people who don't use a pattern will most likely enjoy their design if they know what they are doing.

Conclusion

As paper quilling involves numerous complicated tasks to create designs, it is best to read this guide to learn how to go about the entire process.

Beginners should first endeavor to make different coiled circles in multiple sizes before deciding to create other circles. Additionally, paper quilling is a fun paper craft way to build your creativity level.

Quilled artworks are decorated mainly with attractive aggrandizement that makes for a beautiful paper quilled design. Paper quillers can create different paper quilling designs, including jewelry, cards, frames, and so much more.

Kids and adults can easily engage in this art and make mouth-watering paper quilling designs for friends and family members. The supplies needed for these designs are majorly cheap, which is a great motivation for beginner quillers.

At this point, you should have learned everything about paper quilling and how to create 20 different paper quilling designs.

Happy quilling, quillers!!!

www.ingramcontent.com/pod-product-compliance
Lightning Source LLC
Chambersburg PA
CBHW062033120526
44592CB00036B/2012